Living Stone

YVONNE WEEKES

UK BOOK PUBLISHING

LIVING STONE

Yvonne Weekes was born in London to Montserratian parents and grew up in London and Montserrat; she currently resides in Barbados. She is a writer, arts educator and academic whose research practices and activism utilises theatre and film making, poetry and performance. Yvonne is the recipient of several awards including, Outstanding Director at the First Caribbean Secondary Schools Drama Festival (1992); the Frank Collymore Literary Endowment Award in 2025 for her memoir *Volcano* published by Peepal Tree Press (2006) and published in Spanish by La Pequeña in 2024 and Best Director – Fiction for her first short film *Grief* in 2019. In 2024, the government of Montserrat awarded her the Order of Excellence for her contribution to Arts, Culture and Education. Yvonne Weekes has a PhD in Education from the University of the West Indies. She has taught at the Barbados Community College and the University of the West Indies, Cave Hill Campus.

First published in Great Britain in 2025 by

UK BOOK PUBLISHING INC

Copyright © *Yvonne M S Weekes*, 2025

All Rights Reserved

The right of Yvonne Weekes to be identified as the author of this work has been asserted in accordance with the Copyright, Design and Patents Acts of 1988; all rights reserved.

This book is subject to the condition that no part of this book is to be reproduced, transmitted in any form or means; electronic or mechanical, stored in a retrieval system, photocopied, recorded, scanned, or otherwise. Any of these actions require the proper written permission of the author.

Author Photo by Risée Chadderton Charles

Also by Yvonne Weekes

POETRY
Nomad
Pandemic Moments (with Howard Fergus)

PROSE
Volcano (a memoir)

DRAMA
Blue Soap (in Emancipation Moments edited by Rawle Gibbons)

EDITED BY YVONNE WEEKES
Newton Unsilenced: Narratives Imagined
Voices: Monologues & Dramatic Text for Caribbean Actors
Disasters Matter: Disaster Matters (with Wendy McMahon)

Living Stone is dedicated

To

My Precious Jewels - Nina, Tyler and Nova

CONTENTS

Part One
Back Story 1
    My Fears 2
    Jumbie 3
    Dusk 4
    School Days 5
    Parent Teacher Conference 6
    Stone Heart 7
    Faith 8
    Choking 9
    Christmas Eve 10
    Dry Place 11
    Grandmothers 13
    Golden Flowers 14
    Present 16
    One Day 17
    They Were Playing In The Rain 18

Part Two
A World Inside Out 19
    Stones 20
    In The Deep 22
    Remembering Hugo 23
    Wait 25
    Lashes 26
    The Apocalypse 27
    Pause 29
    A Dream 30
    The Woman Tongue 32
    Jaguar 33
    Just So 34
    Soraya 35
    Gunslinger 36
    Later 38
    Memories 39
    Shells 40

Part Three
Let The Ancestors Pass 41
    Newton 42
    Solace 43
    Grief 44
    Pass 45
    Uncle Joseph 46
    Just Another Day 47

When Our Road Changes	48
Pearls	52
Pearls II	53
Grief II	54
Wake	55
Wishes	57
The Ruler	59
When A Poet Dies	60
Returning	61
Back Story	62
Stone Prayer	64

Acknowledgements **65**

Glossary **66**

Ezekiel 36:26 NIV
I will give you a new heart and put a new spirit in you; I will remove from you your heart of stone and give you a heart of flesh.

Matthew 7:9-11 NIV
Which of you, if your son asks for bread, will give him a stone? Or if he asks for a fish, will give him a snake?

LIVING STONE

PART ONE

BACK STORY

Memories of our lives, our weeks, and our deeds will continue in others
- Rosa Parks

My Fears

I am not afraid to close eyelids
of the dead, to open stiffened fingers,
sculpting them into hands of prayer,
my face covered by sticky spider webs.
The smell of fresh soil thrown on caskets.

I am afraid of poets who strangle
each other with hidden metaphors,
men who strangle women with bare hands,
babies strangled by women after birth,
parents strangled by words fierce like hurricanes.

Incensed smoke blocking broad brimmed hats.
Tuneless hymns sung by men in polyester suits.
Faces paled by unforgiving tears
or snots and tissue bits stuck to faces,
these, do not frighten me.

But I am afraid
of -
gossip picking at my bones,
smiles plucking out my eyes,
hugs suffocating my soul,
handshakes crushing my dreams,
of kisses too, swallowing my life.

Jumbie

It crept on her velvet quiet,
like how jumbie creep in graveyard,
like how snake slither between wet grass,
and mossy stones by a standpipe.
In the glare of the sun,
her blindness clears,
just so.

And just so,
she realised after all these years,
she had not only disappeared
to all those around her.

Just so,
she had become invisible
even to herself.

Dusk

I am searching for my voice
and wish I could listen to only
birds chirping in the evening,
sea's tide turning and churning,
my grandchildren's footsteps running
up my sixty-seven steps, maybe hear the silence
of my tears filling and flowing into myself.

But how to find the light within me?
In the noise of the sirens, the barking
of dogs, the complaining and groaning
about plastic bags and prices rising
and everybody's else's breathing.
I am praying for my voice-
       as I iron my clothes in this empty house.

School Days

The overhead train shakes
my mother's ornaments,
panda cars crawl the streets,
police arrest my epileptic brother.
Sell by date gone,
I stuff a bread loaf
with text books into my bag,
and long for one smiling face
along these cracked up streets.
I live with blue lips, smoky
hate-filled pubs, sus laws, shivering
bodies on pavements near churches.
Muddy waters cover my shoes,
and the wind whips up my skirt.
Pebbles of ice and pigeon shit
fall into my afro as I run
under Hornsey bridge
through the chill.
These memories
have no clear skies
mountains
blue seas
sunrises
not even a piece of star.

Parent Teacher Conference

I asked my father once,
why he married my mum
once a golden bronze
elegant beauty, now bent.
He told me he didn't want
a bastard child.

                    Years later

I watched, embarrassed
my mother's leaking boots.
Saw too, other fathers sitting
at teachers' desks. Wondered
might there be benefits
of being born a bastard?

Stone Heart

You were not there when kicking shadows
frightened me, when dark winter afternoons
covered me after school, when mother's tears
became stone. We bathed in Tottenham's public baths
and dashed through icicle snow, our snot and tears
in drowning cold. My young hands became icicle hard,
washing dishes in British Home stores' restaurant.

The sky barely broke into a sunshine.
The milkman had mercy on Mother's empty
purse and gave us extra bottles of milk.
The paraffin heater choked us, and the stripping
wallpaper's images of Aladdin were no comfort.
All my wishes did not bring you back to us.
My feet were on cold linoleum, you weren't there.

Faith

Sometimes you want to believe that he have regret,
that he feel shame that he don't even know what school
you went to. That he goin remember he children birthday.
You want to believe that he feel some kind of remorse,
all the while he was living high in the sky in Richmond Hill,
you and you four siblings did live down Tottenham Hale
and ain't have no hot water.
No bathroom.
No inside toilet.

You hear the pastor say every Sunday that you is to keep
no record of wrong doings and that you is to have faith
but I feel I real wasting time on he with this faith thing.
Watch me.
Hear this.
He going soon cock up he two foot like Peter Ben
donkey. I don't know neither Peter Ben nor his donkey.
But, I hear my MaMa Honey Fox say it every day.
She used to say too, *please, do the Lord bless you,*
don't waste your faith on no worthless man.
No woman ain't going to heaven anyway,
on account of man. Dem is all Hitler.

Choking

I wake up,
consider that I never see my mother crying,
she who husband left she one cold morning
without warning, who watch fires cremating
she grandchildren, whose lazy sons still disappointing
she. She, who watch she sisters party dem life to the grave,
look neither wary nor weary
when she own mother went into the sky,
no tears, except in church when de spirit tek
she. I just here considering
where all those tears hiding
while she body wasting away
and I here in the morning sun
grieving?

Christmas Eve

Christmas Eve, my mum spent time counting change,
pennies stretched across a bright rug.
Paper bags with curtains and gifts were arranged
among the tinsel sparkling on golden trinkets.
A white angel topped our snowy tree placed
in the alcove close to the glowing electric fire.
Ham on the stove, we children licked her cake bowls.
Years later, I learned of my mother's quiet warring
amidst our Christmas glee. I learned, too,
of all my father's women, of other siblings
my father fathered in hot distant lands.
It was a Christmas Eve when I, a mother myself,
noticed my mother's tired hands seasoning the turkey,
the gold chain around her neck turning black.

Dry Place

Why do these memories come at all?
Appearing like a lost stranger
unannounced on your veranda?
Or like black birds screeching
on your rooftop and scratching
the galvanize?
Like rope tightening
around your neck, rainbow breaking
though your class window, making
your tears fall just so?

Memory is Penny Lane.
Mother's bathroom curtain of the Queen.
Construction men cat calling you in the rain.
Who really ask these memories to come?
Who asked them to unravel your day?
And you've tried
so hard to stay away
from that place.
That place you used to call home
where your navel string
was incinerated.
That place.
The scent
of dead people and ganja.

From the time you reach Heathrow or Gatwick,
one siren cracks open
memories running through broken black
faces that take you back to Tottenham riots.

I wonder why these memories
won't go away.
Stay away.
Keep away.
Shit.
You try to strap
down your heart.
Even when you return
to calming seas, they sink
like stone in your throat,
can't stay away.

Memories twist you inside out
and all these years,
they're still scrawling
through your insides,
mercilessly scalding
your heart, bubbling
burn in your throat,
writhing, writing
themselves into poems.

Grandmothers

"You too force ripe!"
The girl stuffed her empty chest with balls of toilet paper.

"You think you is a woman?"
The girl recognized an odour between her MaMa's thighs
she did not have.

"You really smelling yourself!"
The girl hid in the school bathroom while the blood seeped
into her white panties.

"If you talk to boys, you'll get pregnant."
The girl lost her laughter as she walked to school.
Her nerves stiffening.

The girl recalls these women, supposedly her blood—
one dragging her bare feet up mountains of cotton fields,
living her life unafraid of dark nights and jumbies,
sad about nothing, not even the man she called 'Hitler';
the other baking her own bread, dressed in black trousers,
refusing to make herself any man's wife.

A big woman now, she walks between their two stone crosses.
    She laughs.
        These women were some serious wretches.

Golden Flowers

She remembered the grandmother
light, fair, or maybe bronze -
called a 'red woman' by some.
At Christmas, she enjoyed sitting
on the grandmother's patio,
listening to the firefly buzzing their ears,
watching the revellers throng and wine
to masqueraders' music, iron band
and reggae beats in the streets below.

One day the grandmother bought her a hat.
It was a beautiful straw hat
with golden yellow flowers -
        golden just like the grandmother.

You must wear it whenever you're in the sun.
Don't let me catch you walking in the sun.
You can't afford to get any blacker.
Don't let me see you without that hat now.

After that, those times on the grandmother's patio
felt like her skin was just crackling
to the music of the masqueraders.
Fireflies really hurt her eyes. She wanted to party
with revellers in hot midday sun.

One day, while contemplating life,
she saw a lizard crawling in front of her path
behind the back of her house. She followed
as it raised its neck, moving slowly towards
water trickling around mossy standpipe
stones.
She took the hat in her hand
and stomped it joyously,
crushing the yellow golden flowers.

The next Christmas she didn't watch the fête
from the patio.
She became the masquerade.

Present

I thank my God every day
for my son - Nathan Emanuel Gibbons,
who tells his daughter
she can be whatever
she wants to be, even
the lizard in the moon on top
of her gran gran's house,
gives his son light kisses,
sits in the sun with his three children.

This is the man who teaches me
that a father can be
soft
warm
loving
trustworthy
present.

One Day

All that I am leaving my son:
boxes full of books,
love letters tied with purple ribbons,
too many cups gifted by students,
cards of encouragement by church sisters,
wild notes written in between hurricanes,
suicides, divorce, volcanic eruptions,
broken dates, missed journeys at airports;
dark poems with too many adjectives,
old photos of crisp confirmation clothes,
journals written during morning prayers
sipping fever grass and aniseed teas
under hanging wind chimes.
I pray that these ghosts,
my only valuables
will sustain him
when I am silent.

They Were Playing in the Rain

I said, "Come out of the rain, my precious jewels."

"Not precious jewels, Gran Gran. Wet jewels.

I am gold

Nina is diamond

Nova is Pearl

Daddy is Iron

Mummy is Amethyst

And you're Emerald, Gran Gran."

And that's how Tyler named us

And that's how I call them.

PART TWO

A WORLD INSIDE OUT

Stones

My life is a series of prayers and stones.
Burdens and stories and stone victories,
laughter, stones, exploding waterfalls
broken into stones, sunken mountains,
scattered stones in dark waters
swallowing up memories and city stones.
Mother. Father. Sister. Cousins.
Ancestors crossing murky waters,
some into slave ships,
tongues heavy like stone.

My father followed my mother - Catherine
to England lands, no gold, just grey stone.
Come slaving in factories, no golden streets,
blistered fingers swelling in cotton factories
like lime fields, same clearing of stone
till bodies turn to stone self - to rock stone
minds turn to rock stone - hearts turn to rock stone -
life turn to grey rock stone in Hackney's
blistering fog chimneys filling my parents' lungs.

My siblings and I, brown and black babies
hug wire meshes, crave peace but feared
being torn into pieces in playgrounds, white
nurseries, and thrown into Thames black
waters, but now these stories and stones
smashing my prayers and memories on rock stone -
on black sand - grey cities - hateful
priests - sisters' treacheries - coral rock stone

false men - Satan/s smashing dreams,
   temptations sweet like Bajan dumplings.
     Lovers whose love are more like stones
        than scrambled eggs.

Hurricanes
     hit like stones
wintery hail   cane fires
    deaths   suicides   babies
with no tomorrows.

   All that is left -

   clocks standing still
   brittle bones
   cemeteries
  cold chalices
  dark secrets
  misty memories
  lost letters.

And as my MaMa Honey Fox
   might say,
  who de rock stone really
   cares so long de sun rises and falls,
   that you do not have enough grips,
   suitcases, valises, handbags,
   and boxes to hold all your prayers and stones?

In the Deep

There is a tourist sea
and then there is **our** sea,
darker than the pools of my own eyes,
a sea which spits vomit
over fishermen's boats
lands sargassum atop ancient roofs,
expels the plastics of our lives
with sand over potholed streets.
This wild warlike sea, crazy
with no respect even for the holy,
sinking our lives without mercy,
exposing our salty misery,
comes through our cities
without even so much as a wind
to hold it back down, and all
now my blood running
cold, and I am wondering
how big is the ocean to hold
so many boats and ghosts?

Remembering Hugo

So, all day she notes:
the weight of the sun,
dogs crouching at doors,
shirtless men hammering,
fat babies sleeping
through plywood sawing,
through squeals and innocent screams
of village children.

The incessant mooing of cows
reverberates through chicken coops
and cocks' crow as if they know
the dream day was coming to an end.
Women hum soft tunes
packing corned beef, sardines, and Crix.
All along some disbelieving villagers
fooled by the quiet day, clouds ascending,
sit in the cool, in the stillness,
sipping Heineken with fried chicken wings,
ignoring the butterflies swarming around,
dismissing, too, stammering voices on the radio
announcing the early September hurricane.
Into the haze of the afternoon, little girls
rest between sticky thighs, while mothers
grease patterns for the new world of school.

Then night falls.

She - the mother - hears the trees breathe.
The rising evil of the wind prevents sleep.

Why the moon watching her and her child so?
In the darkness and in her fear,
she hears the wind part the red galvanized roof:
tears drip, while swelling winds like mallets
grind everything down and away. The sky
over her bed moves her to a clothes cupboard,
seven family members already packed in there.
She crouches with child in arms.
Fear empties her stomach onto the floor.
The rain like needles falls on her neck,
drip drip. She keeps her eyes shut.
Winds shatter furniture as Hugo passes.

Morning comes.

Crickets, too.
Light reveals
everything skin-out in the yard,
corned beef, sardines, and Crix
lie next to the shrinking dogs, cows, chickens.
Traumatized trees wrap around houses,
their naked roots exposed.
The 'eye' goes and will not come back.
All is broken.
The bones of birds clothe the earth.
She sees the staggering house,
escapes to sleep in car untouched,
yet, drowning in leaves.

What comfort
is the sun, now warm light,
if leaves lay too wet,
to wrap her child tight?

Wait

At ninety-eight, my Tantan died quietly
after living life unconcerned and leisurely,
sipping her Stone's Ginger Wine slowly.
She was a free woman. Free from pain,
husband long gone to sea and son
who left island long before I was born.
We couldn't find the son to tell him,
"Your mother's dead." We washed her body
in the same wooden house that survived Hugo.

The volcano was spewing, and the ash
blowing reached the north of the island.
There were no funeral homes then.
I put the sheer white stockings
on her cold feet while cousin Laurene
pulled the silver comb through her hair.
We understood how Jesus' disciples felt.
We all - Pearl, Edna, Selina - threaded stories
about her as sunrays came through the shutters.

Pearl slipped
a silken scarf
around her neck.
We waited, coughing
through the dust
for the funeral car
to arrive.

Lashes

Sulphur choked clouds in the sky,
birds flapped their wings, grey
from stone fragments
which fell into my eyes.
There and then I knew
rivers overflow
spirits journey
history repeats
justice is invisible
death is marble
Sulphur follows
grief does not sing
old wounds sometimes,
do not heal.

The Apocalypse

And then one day
suddenly the buildings trembled as if to cry.
Tears filled up gullies, flowed
through parishes, overflowed villages,
swept towns and streets,
washed away sargassum,
put out burning cane.
People began to weep, too.
They didn't recognize their island.
Six young women shopping for dresses,
burnt alive.
A mother fixing her hair, murdered
with her children present.
A baker, counting the nights savings,
shot at close range.

All that blood began to meander
into supermarkets and spas
beach boutiques and bars
rum shops and restaurants
breakfast parties and fêtes,
swept up working girls near District A,
coiled round Queens Park, licking down
all locked doors of The Central Bank.
Tears and blood meeting each other
flowed down the heights into terraces,
through cul-de-sacs and gated communities,
developments, the sea ports and airport.
Leaves lost their sway as bloody tears

rose reaching the floors of glass elevators,
people began drowning in the smell of blood.
They watched voiceless
until everything began to collapse
into the raging seas.

Pause

whether gun
is silencer
protector
instrument of war
friend of gang member
or sign of death rattler
a big man toy in the litter
of little boys' hands
daggers untamed in childhood games

neither pitcher of water
nor pause can cool down
these senseless killers
        we return to bacchanalia

A Dream

And so, I sleep, fitfully night after night
heavy lids while the streetlights shine
through my bedroom window, curtains
create ghostly shapes of the leafy lots,
everyone sleeps. Sometimes the moon joins
the streetlights to glare at our homes,
casting shadows.

I recall the time when a boy
came over my wall silently, in broad day
like a mist, with gun shots to the face, leaving
a trail of blood, across our adjoining walls.
Not a sound could be heard, not rustling
of our sheets, towels hanging and blowing,
not a single word from the dog
revealed his presence.

I see again negro dogs sniffing for his blood,
and in my dreams, slave hunters chase him
through bushes, terror in his breathing.
They throw him into a sack gagged and bound,
just like the guards who'll hurl him
into a prison cell. There is water –
in my dream, rising –
a mother throws her son,
still weaning, to smiling fish who gouge his eyes,
bleeding the sea red.
Not once in my sleep

can I save the boy
whose face opens wider from police bullets.
I wake then,
> hearing the neighbour's dog barking.

        I cannot swim.

The Woman Tongue

Speaks of dead slaves,
prayers and sorrows,
our sores oozing puss,
our men's necks snapping,
babies birthed in wretched cane fields.

Yet, no matter how the woman tongue shakes,
she cannot speak of beloved babies' hearts
sinking from chained hurt into dark waters,
expelled from drinking a cool cup of cider root,
blood quietly washed away
while women return unrattled
to their scarred normal lives,
tongues holding pods of silence.

Jaguar

In the soft leather smell of the seats
the leaves of the manchineel trees
fought against the rumbling seas.
She watched a single drop of misty water
land against the forested windscreen.
When his fingers clawed her knees
hope flew into a slice of light.
The sun fell into the black sand.
Suddenly, he withdrew his teeth
and the ignition purred again.
    She wished she had waited for her father's
car to pick her up.
    Trembling, she pressed down the pleats of her skirt.
He dropped her home, safely.

Just So

And what is a stone good for? Stone does just be lying
between wet grass and people flowers, ain't troubling
nobody. Just so, somebody see de stone lying
still, hard and useless pan de ground pan a morning,
after a cool little walk. Fast so, stone lying
in somebody house. Some use it as door stopper.
Some use it to scrub them foot bottom in the bath.
Some use it to hold down papers, stop them from mash up
dem valuable tings in the wind. But, ir/regardless
of all these uses, the stone is a common thing
all about the place- in park, on road, in sand, just lying,
in a gutter. Even in your own yard and mek you stump
you toe. And dis common ting, a stone, dat ain't trouble
a soul, end up lodged in a woman head – just so.

Soraya

In a ditch filled with sand,
they stoned her for cooking meals for another man.
No Jesus to save her,
unlike Mary Magdalene, who slept with men.

Now they stone her for:
sassiness,
sexiness,
a sharp brain,
sweet smile,
smart ways.
They wished they could stone her, without censor,
consequence,
without quite killing her.
Or, just bury her in dark cane
where not even the slave master's overseer will find her.

  Cover her with a stone.
        A large stone.

Gunslinger

*"And when my heart is overwhelmed,
lead me to the rock that is higher than I,
that is higher than I".*

He come home cool so.
She has no will to fight.
He pounces on her
unzips his trousers
fires through her body,
his lips tobacco coarse
her heart overwhelmed.
If only she could reach
the fillet knife close by
caress his broad shoulder
puncture a hole close to the jugular
watch his mouth open wide
as he falls sliding off the counter,
slice a piece of the dark meat
off his face - all cowboys have scars -
        watch it sizzle in the hot frying pan.

He shakes off himself
returns his trigger.
She wipes her hand slowly
across the once fire red lipstick,
fumbles for the high heeled shoes,
prays as she smooths down her skirt.
Where this God hiding
his face while her brain nightly concussing?

Later, she scrubs her tongue
sees her reflection in the shiny faucet
notices no moon watching.
                    Where is her rock?

Later

He runs her bath water
warm,
smelling of lavender
zesty pink grapefruit.

He removes her night dress
soft
aching left shoulder sinks
into warm water.

He continues smiling,
"Lily!"
She hears his affection
he strokes her gently.

But he's punched the sound
clean
from her bleeding ears.
Sorry won't fix them.

And no sorry stops
blood
filling her stomach
in grapefruit-lavender-water.

While she's dying,
He's still saying:
"Lily Love."

Memories

Like a shadow under the house, they always come
through my window. Rape me, then go 'bout their business.
Nobody believe me, 'cause they say I mad. They come through mist,
rainy season, summer breeze. I don't feel nothing 'cause I am dead.

One time they come through fire, burnished orange with red flames.
There was smoke everywhere. My silk dress melts while they
raped me. But they say I mad. Force long needle into my arm,
hold me down, 'bout four of dem. They say it will stop my dreams.

Sometimes, they slip through the cracks under my door.
They think I am a proper fool. Yet, I see their faces.
The drying leaves in my hair, the smell of salt and sulphur
on my breath does not stop them. They still come.

I wish the sea down the road would save me.
I see it foaming through the nut tree and the misty sky.
I don't get no flowers. Just twenty-five cents tossed
on the kitchen table next to the oil lamp.

In the morning these fragments will come
draped like the spider's web covering
the peephole of my wooden door,
for which there is no key.

Shells

Could not keep on watching
babies wrapped in swaddling cloth,
Mothers covered in polka dot blood. I lie
comfortably on my front room couch, listening
to some radio pastor preach of Israel's lamenting
about the promised land, and I wonder if Moses
still climbs up the mountain, he hears the grumbles
through the manna of wailing.

One small boy standing on a single crutch, right leg missing
rummages rubble for bread, but finds bullet shells.

Lemon and olive trees downed, detonated sewers
encircle a Gaza mosque, the prayers of bare feet men
huddled in shard glass, rise up to the dusty faces
on a crumbling bridge and a hospital shredded by Israeli bombs.

A dog carries a limp cat in its mouth, digs a hole to bury it.

One news reporter barely misses being crushed by falling
chunks.

Hāshim ibn Abd Manāf, descendant of Prophet Muḥammad
turns in his grave, while the death toll worms its way through
Instagram, Facebook, WhatsApp. Even car radios talk of dying
not killing.
                      Palestine reaches my sleep, grabs
        my praying hands.
                          While my own weeping imagines
                ascending clouds as gravestones.

PART THREE

LET THE ANCESTORS PASS

Newton

While others unearth
our unnamed bones
our dog teeth
with cowry charms,
bronze bangles,
clay pipes,
refashioning our stories,
we must remember
that even dead memories
pounded by sun
worn out by pain
refuse silence,
ready to speak.

Solace

On any moonless night, it is said a woman alone,
can be seen walking with a hole in the middle of her chest.
Her tongue parched, is stuck to the roof of her mouth.
The fireflies light up the scar on her shoulder.

There is supernatural darkness where a heart should be.
When she passes, sulphur flows through her nostrils.
The frogs are awakened by her presence as her feet touch
the earth. She looks for her loved ones' graves, eyes
searching and cannot find them, as their souls will not cross
the seas to come to her. The hole in her chest
becomes a river, flowing into a once filled womb.

She finds no solace in anyone's condolences.

Grief

It is easier to write a poem than to grieve,
much easier to google words to rhyme with grief,
easier to create a clever line of toe-curling
assonance. Even when it lands alone, balled
up in a dark corner the poem, like a cat,
rises easily, to make what is visible
to ordinary people, messy.

But grief, hates music, shudders in sun,
wrings your soul case, fills you with sleeplessness
leaves the tongue parched with tears
while worms crawl underneath fingertips.
When the pastor's asks, "death where is your sting?"
bile seeps into the mouth and brings no meaning.

Pass

Midday
some jumbie find her,
hanging clothes.
The smell of fried jack fish
wafting jewelled memories.
Cob weaving silk
webbing across her eyes
her nose
her lips
brings an old sadness
to her stone heart.
So, under the spider's weft
drifting from the clothesline
she stands
        casted.

Let's her ancestor pass.

Uncle Joseph

I ask my uncle for his email.

He says: josephweekes@gmail.com

It is a random name. Never heard before.

Disconnected from my memories

of him. "Where you get that name from?"

He says, "a me nyame, gal". Joseph.

"But why they call you Everton, then?"

"Gal, ah me jumbie nyame, yes!"

I now have to reshape our memories. *Joseph*.

Imagine me uncle could a dead,

and me would a never know

dat one jumbie named Joseph

covering me.

Just Another Day

She wakes, night shirt inside out, label to the front.
Ghosts follow her.
      rain
      baby scream
      truck screech
      bird chirp
Morning brings fresh grief.
She's inside out, like the shirt.
Melancholy tunes play on the radio.
Short shadows creep around her bed.
Neighbours go about their daily lives.
Not once will they check to see
if all that is left of her
is her skeletal remains.
Nextdoor holds a birthday
party.
She hears a balloon pop.
She unravels.

When Our Road Changes

1
Aunty Ethel

My aunt died smelling
like White Diamonds.
She loved that fragrance.
She gave me nothing while she lived.
But when she died, her daughter Laurene
gave every woman in the family
a bottle of perfume from her large
collection off the dusty dressing table.
I kept my unnamed green bottle
without ever using it.
Just so, the bottle kept
falling over, on my own
overfilled dresser.

One day, remembering her,
I treated myself to White Diamonds,
threw that annoying bottle away.

2
Uncles

My uncle Organiser, now dead
had one woman and one wife.
Both showed up to my grandmother's funeral.
One had a white wreath with baby breath.
The other had one with every colour flower.
One cried long dry water out her eye.
The other preened throughout the service
like the young yam my uncle called her.

My uncle Everton and I watched.
from a distance, while my Aunty Inez
wailing like a cow in birth,
tried to throw herself
onto my grandmother's casket,
when the men started to throw big
lumps of soil and rock into the hole.

I don't recall the words of the two women.
But their warring could be heard high
among the rising funeral mound
and the Mother's Union off-key Anglican hymns.
I touched my uncle Everton's hand. He flinched.
Everybody now touchy, he said.

That was the day that my family,
without shame became legends
of spectacular funerals.

3
Pearl

My sister Pearl
told me
she lay on
the carpet.
No one could
make her move.

Her child had
just gone to sleep
with the clouds.

Cousin Sean
brought her
Christmas flowers.
She moaned.

I offered nothing
but my
voicelessness.

I wondered
if her tears
reflected in the
snowy window.

4
Aunt Kate

When my paternal grandmother died,
I wore a brown African outfit
with matching head dress woven
with gold, bronze, chocolate threading.

An African girlfriend said it was a traditional dress
of the Ibo people, respect to elders who had passed.
Next week, a local gossip in *Long Grass*
wrote I dressed like a pappy show
to my own grandmother's funeral.
                It was only then that I cried.

Pearls

Leave your pearls at her door,
        lie quietly on her cold floor,
                carry no flowers,
                      offer no platitudes,
                            speak in hushed tones,
                      while the nuthatches
          screech into her sacred darkness.
Let your stillness be her prayers.

Pearls II

They offered me prayers
that didn't fill my heart,
eye water leaking into a basket
that should have contained bread.

They offered me condolences
that couldn't perfume my sour breath
filling the church air.
They could have just offered tea.

They offered me flowers
that my vases couldn't contain.
Putrid water calloused my heart,
which their holiness couldn't see.

They were afraid to dance in the rain with me
with their pearled necklines and church eyes.
They didn't know how to shoo away the ghosts
who came to me day and night.

Their gods were too high up.
They didn't know.
                    Stones don't comfort.

Grief II

The girl woke up. Looked up to the heavens
for a dance to lift her sinking soul. Literally looked
up for a melody a sign. She saw only the dead, dread,
daring eyes of friends and lovers, she once danced
with. They danced around her bed every morning.
If only she could point her toes, they would perhaps
leave their round around her bed. But by night fall
her toes had curled into a comma. Instead of the breath
of life in her navel strumming, death's punch stopped her.
In the darkness of the room, she couldn't do flat
back to dance away the interruptions to her life.
The curve in her back carried a basket of tears.
Her fingers were numb with pain. They were blunt,
not soft. She was waiting for a beat   a pause   a tune
a note in the face of the melting moonlight. A cock
crowing in the distance did not provide the solace
she needed. The clock ticked mercilessly, the whirring
of the AC did not frighten these dead dancers. None
of these rhythms could provide the music she needed
to keep the dead away, even the streetlight flowing
into her room was no solace.
                              She could not dance.

Wake

For James William Allen

In the midnight shadows
my mother covers the mirrors with white cloths.
Light flecks through coal fires.
I sit on my grandmother's steps
surrounded by languages of mourning women.
Men murmuring in the yard cut throats
of pig and goat, while a headless chicken
flies up into the breadfruit tree.
Fireflies gather back and forth.
I hold my breath.

More women in head ties come into the yard,
peeping on the dead. They pull tablecloths
from cardboard boxes, peel cassava,
and sweet potatoes on the steps,
chop onions, garlic, and sweet peppers,
wash rice and chop skinned meats.

Later, I'm screaming
while women scrub my body
with the same blue bar,
that washed
down my grandfather's body,
in the galvanised shower
surrounded by bloody meats and animal faeces.
Scrubbed clean and dressed,
my uncles lift my body, pass me over the table.
I peer through my fingers at my fearless siblings

as one-by-one they are passed over our grandfather.
It feels like a stone in my throat.

I hide in the corner of the room,
watch my grandfather's body on a table.
I see shak shaks, ukulele, two guitars.
His dark suit, black shoes,
and fedora lay on a chair,
blue soap, enamel basin on the floor.

I turn my head to the candles, close my eyes,
refusing to see my grandfather and his ghost.
  Men drum,
    chant songs I don't know.
  Among the anguished breathing
  and hum of rocking women,
              I close myself from what is yet to come.

Wishes

How I imagine the story behind closed doors.
Blackie was my friend.

Blackie stand bold pan de Hothersall Road
every day God make Sunday
in front de neighbour gate smoking ganja.
        De wife a wait for he fix up de place,

repair de countertop, rip off de old shingles, paint de canteen.

At least do some real work.
        He say,
        I work hard. I always put all the money on the table.
Laziness never kill a soul.

Sometimes, he sit 'cross de same road pan a metal chair
wid some young men. Old man like he, selling cut cane,
peanuts, and breadfruit from somebody tree.
        He outside in he marina, gold chain
swinging like he a gangster.

        De wife watch he from de shop, wish
he would come off the road.
        He tell her,
    but I put all my money on you table.
He big belly skinning he teeth wid every woman dat pass
in they fancy car stopping traffic. Police never once stop he except
to buy some force ripe mangoes he get from a neighbour back yard.

Blackie ain't 'cross de road no more, and for the first time in
years everybody can see through the cut down bougainvillea.
The neighbour chain link clear clear like silver dollar,
and on a piece of wood de sign:
> *Absolutely NO Trespassing!*

Blackie young Rasta friends spruce up
de piece of shop
wid fresh paint. Dem tie a piece of
black cloth round the shop,
> and a sign say:
> *R I P UP DAY.*

Ain't no comfort to her, especially now
he fall down just so
in front de people dem chain link.
> Look how he ain't dead two minutes
before de neighbour put up a sign saying:
> *Absolutely NO Trespassing!*
> Dat man got de nerve to dead just so,
give dat woman 'cross de road she wishes.

The Ruler

For Edith Bellot Allen

I wish I could begin life again,
large white handkerchief in pocket,
though honestly, I have no memory
of ever having used one, it seemed
a frivolous thing, always discarded.

Besides a teary snot,
can a handkerchief, wipe away bloody cloths,
refugees' miseries bombs ripping broken skies,
long lines of emaciated families,
strutting gilded carriages to carry King and Mistress,
holy water blessed?

If, there is a handkerchief, with such potency
to remove troubled memories, I would surely
not get my knuckles
smacked by my insistent teacher
long gone into her own sky.

When A Poet Dies

For Sir Howard Fergus

First. The sea,
angry and wild, pushes
over the charred land,
butterflies drift
through thyme
gardens,
easily caught by hand.

Storms stop breezes,
trees bend against
black sands.

Second. The words.
Letters lay on an empty shelf,
no teeth or lips or tongue
to call them out, no vowels,
no scathing consonants.
Rhyme silenced.
              Imagery vanished.
                          Tone dead.

Finally.
How to make sense of this?
No ink can cast his words
into possible worlds.

Returning

For Ellyn "Calypsonian Hurricane Ellen" Stanton

For five minutes I touched her face,
said *thank you I love you*
and then stepped away.
I watched the casket go
into the furnace.
The curtain was drawn.
They said *it takes four*
hours for a body to burn.
On the way home,
I imagined the flames
on your white skin.

Driving home from the crematorium,
I saw my body going into soft, dark soil
among small stones and twigs,
purple roses falling on me,
my spirit floating up to the sky.
Later, I'd come down sweetly,
forcing my way back into some day,
returning between memories
of me that you haven't kept.
A lily in a pond of another land,
some day.

Back Story

So maybe the scar on my shoulder scares men away.
Maybe the moon doesn't shine in my dark cave.
I don't give a damn
once thunder claps close by,
I am the lightening of your shadows.
        Jump! In fear.
Lizards follow me around the shower.
No perfume can cover my sulphur hair.
I spit cou cou out my mouth, reminder
of my father's cornmeal porridge.
My knees black, scuffed,
kneel on coral soil for my own sins.
        Prayers to keep you away.
Once someone tried to tie down
the wildness in me.
Tried to stretch me invisible.
Muffle my dreams and poems.
        Where is he now?
So maybe you can't tell my mixed-up tongue.
Neither British or Montserratian or Bajan
because I come from no place at all.

Yet, I am rock
made of volcano rock
        living on a small rock.
              Pelt your rocks.
        I reject your rocks in Jesus' name.

Buzz of flies circle my red locks.
I hear your whispers even in silence.
I am a complicated Christian girl. So tired.
But, like the *jammet* I am underneath,
I'll just speak my truth in language
that perhaps only Kamau will understand.
Whether from some place or no place
death's light hand frees us all.

Stone Prayer

This is mine:
fingers be soft healing,
kind eyes revealing hearts of flesh.
In this world of mourning, my breath
be Jesus' showering love.
                          Tears be candescent
clear. Rainfall eases me.

My prayer
is also for those whose spines remained unbent
in the long care-giving. Who knew there would be dying,
and they would be dying,
and there would be so much dying,
and that dying would be beguiling?
We were all masked, but they were taken
anyway. Pray my heart
remains singing among this unreal dying.

And we couldn't gather for any of this dying.
Their caskets came through on my TV.

I saw only dark fireflies on my patio   **y**
                                              l
                                   f

ACKNOWLEDGEMENTS

All praise to God from whom all the creative talent flows.

I would like to give thanks to my wonderful sister/friend Loretta Collins Klobah for her indefatigable patience and unparalleled mentorship.

I'm grateful to all the people who read this manuscript along the way. For their love, input, critique, advice and encouragement. Kerry Belgrave, Robert Sandiford, Lafleur Cockburn-Jackman, Jacinth Howard, Anthony Joseph, Bartosz Wojcik and the team at UK Publishing.

Love and blessings to my son Nathan who always believes in my writing. For my daughter in law, Tanisha as well as Sheena Rose and Mathew Clarke for their input and their excellent creative 'eyes'.

Grateful acknowledgment is also made to the following print and online publications, in which certain poems in this collection appear in slightly modified form or with slightly altered titles:

Pandemic Moments, "Grief II" (p79) and "Stone Prayer" (p. 78) in Fergus Publishing, 2021.

Arts Etc, "Grief" first appeared May 19, 2020 on https://www.artsetcbarbados.com/

Caribbean Childhood Traumas and Triumphs: in Interviewing the Caribbean Vol 5 UWI Press, 2020. "Golden Flowers" (pp.138-139).

Disaster Matters: Disasters Matter, "Remembering Hugo" (pp.21-22) House of Nehesi Publishers, 2021.

Glossary

Jumbie. Ghost or Spirit referred to in Caribbean stories and folklore.

Force Ripe. Older people in Montserrat use this term to explain that a young girl or boy is growing up too quickly.

Smelling Yourself. A young girl who is behaving as if she is a big woman. Probably a reference to the fact that the girl has not even had a menstrual period as yet. Smelling yourself and Force Ripe are sometimes used interchangeably.

Masqueraders. Costumed Carnival Characters who dance at special festivals.

The Woman Tongue. This tree's name comes from the Arabic plant 'laebach'. When agitated by the wind, the pods and enclosed seeds are said to produce an incessant rattle likened to a woman's chatter.

Newton. This is a reference to the Newton Slave Burial Ground which is the largest and earliest slave burial ground discovered in Barbados. Here lie the remains of nearly six hundred enslaved men, women and children who toiled and suffered through brutal plantation slavery. It is a site of painful memories.

Touchy. A made-up word for someone being overly sensitive.

Long Grass. A column which used to appear in the Montserrat Reporter. It used to highlight frivolous and political gossip. In Montserrat culture Long Grass Long grass is actually an annoying bush commonly associated with being a gossipmonger.

Pappy show. Showing off but looking like a fool or joker in the person's eyes.

Jumbie Nyame. There is an old tradition in Montserrat of naming new born babies with the name of a dead ancestor, jumbie name.

Jammet. Perceived as a shameless and brash woman.

www.ingramcontent.com/pod-product-compliance
Lightning Source LLC
Chambersburg PA
CBHW041306240426
43661CB00011B/1029